Day and Night

By JoAnne Nelson • Pictures by Ruth Flanigan

PROJECT DIRECTOR: Judith E. Nayer
COVER DESIGN: Elaine A. Groth

Published by Modern Curriculum Press

 Modern Curriculum Press, Inc.
A division of Simon & Schuster
13900 Prospect Road, Cleveland, Ohio 44136

Copyright © 1990 by McClanahan Book Company, Inc. All rights reserved.

This edition is published simultaneously in Canada by
Globe/Modern Curriculum Press, Toronto.

Manufactured in the United States of America. This book or parts thereof may not be reproduced in any form or mechanically stored in any retrieval system without written permission of the publisher.

ISBN 0-8136-4310-4 (STY PK)   ISBN 0-8136-4306-6 (BK)

10 9 8 7 6 5 4   94 93

Goodbye sun, hello moon.
Sun, you went away too soon.

I watched you sink behind the hill.
Are other children playing still?

Where do you go when the moon is high?
Why don't you stay up in the sky?

My side of Earth has turned to night.
Tell me where you shine your light.

I am the sun, I'm far away.
I am the star that makes your day.

I'm in the sky, I make it glow.
My light and warmth help things to grow.

You only think I've gone away.
But it is Earth that turns each day.

Earth is round, just like a ball.
You never feel it move at all.

When your side of Earth turns away from me,
my light shines far across the sea.

The children there play in the light,
while you are sleeping through the night.

Hello sun, goodbye moon.
Sun, you woke me up so soon.

You make the morning glow with light.
Hello dawn, goodbye night.

You make the light, you make the day.
Now I can go outside and play.

I work and play and very soon,
You're overhead, and it is noon.

In the afternoon the day turns cool.
I'm with my friends, it's after school.

Your light grows dim at the end of day.
Soon I must go inside to play.

Now, sun, I see you in the west.
Night will come, and I will rest.

Our side of Earth has turned away.
We're back where we were yesterday.

Hello, moon, it's late, you see.
My bed's the place for me to be.

Day and night, night and day.
I rather like it just this way.